UKRAINIAN-AMERICAN POETS RESPOND

UKRAINIAN-AMERICAN POETS RESPOND

Poets of Queens Press
Yara Arts Group
New York, 2022

Designed and composed by Oleksandr Fraze-Frazenko.
Cover by Waldemart Klyuzko.

© All rights reserved. Printed in The USA. No part of this work may be reproduced or used in any form by any means — graphic, electronic or mechanical, including photocopying, recording, taping or usage in information storage and retrieval systems — without prior written permission of the authors, except for brief extracts for the purpose of review of this book.

ISBN: 978-1-7351478-6-4

CONTENTS

Judith Baumel 9
Julia Kolchinksy Dasbach 10
Lila Dlaboha 18
Boris Dralyuk 27
Anna Frajlich 28
Luba Gawur 30
Bob Holman 32
Eugene Hutz 36
Olena Jennings 38
Ilya Kaminsky 42
Olga Livshin 45
Oksana Lutsyshyna 47
Kristina Lucenko 50
Stash Luczkiw 51
Valya Dudycz Lupescu 53
Vasyl Makhno 56
Oksana Maksymchuk 63
Askold Melnyczuk 68
Nina Murray 72
Krystia Nora 78
Dzvinia Orlowsky 81
Maria G. Rewakowicz 87
Oksana Rosenblum 91
Ksenia Rychtycka 94
Vera Sirota 97
Virlana Tkacz 100
Christina Turczyn 102
Genya Turovskaya 106
Nicole Yurcaba 111

Ukrainian American Poets Respond began with two virtual readings, on March 16 and the other on April 14, 2022. Poets gathered to give their poetic responses to the war Russia waged on Ukraine. In the anthology, we have also included poets who didn't get the chance to participate in the readings. Among those we have Ilya Kaminsky and Eugene Hutz, who gave Kharkiv poet Serhiy Zhadan's words his own twist.

Some of the poets were born in Ukraine and some were born in the United States, making them a diverse group. Their first languages range from English, Ukrainian, Polish, and Russian. Their poetic practices are all based in Ukrainian culture and heritage.

Yara Arts Group, which focuses much of their time in translation of work from Ukrainian for the stage, and Poets of Queens, a reading series and press, collaborated to put together this anthology. Virlana Tkacz, of Yara Arts Group, contributed to the anthology and I represented Poets of Queens in the anthology.

In the *New York Times*, Ilya Kaminsky wrote about the importance of poetry during war. He ends his essay with the lines, "In the middle of war, he is asking for poems," referring to a friend. This war has proved that poetry is necessary.

Poets I have admired from afar and poets I have worked beside are brought together in this anthology. We hope you will join these poets in creating your own work or responding to the call for action in your own way.

Olena Jennings
New York City, 2022

Judith Baumel's books are *The Weight of Numbers*, for which she won The Walt Whitman Award of the Academy of American Poets; *Now*; *The Kangaroo Girl*; *Passeggiate* and *Thorny*. She is Professor Emerita of English and Founding Director of the Creative Writing Program at Adelphi University. She has served as President of The Association of Writers and Writing Programs, director of The Poetry Society of America and a Fulbright Scholar in Italy.

Irij

For now, let us choose not to remember
who said History repeats as Tragedy then Farce,
and who else repeated such nonsense
with variations because, friends, allow me
to be pedantic, just this moment. History repeats
as Tragedy more than once. Many times, in fact.
And Farce appears only briefly in the interacts.
In the main acts we find great and strong
winds that rend the mountains and break
them into pieces. In the main acts we find
earthquakes. In the main acts we find fires.

God passes by all of this and leaves
a still small voice in which we hear
what we need to hear, if anything at all,
and through which we wonder what we
are doing where our mothers and fathers
died and where, before they died, they built
a language that became a nation and that nation
a story and that story a home which we carry
along. It's where the white storks return
from migration to find their nests destroyed
and they are homeless but still protagonists.

    previously published in *The Common*

Julia Kolchinksy Dasbach (www.juliakolchinsky.com) emigrated from Dnipro, Ukraine as a Jewish refugee in 1993, when she was six years old. She is the author of three poetry collections: *The Many Names for Mother*, winner the Wick Poetry Prize (Kent State University Press, 2019), finalist for the Jewish Book Award; *Don't Touch the Bones* (Lost Horse Press, 2020), winner of the 2019 Idaho Poetry Prize; and *40 WEEKS*, forthcoming from YesYes Books in 2023. Her poems appear in *POETRY, Ploughshares, American Poetry Review*, and *The Nation*, among others. She holds an MFA from the University of Oregon and a Ph.D. in Comparative Literature and Literary Theory from the University of Pennsylvania. Her dissertation, *Lyric Witness: Intergenerational (Re)collection of the Holocaust in Contemporary American Poetry*, pays particular attention to the underrepresented atrocity in the former Soviet territories. Julia is the author of the model poem for *"Dear Ukraine": A Global Community Poem* https://dearukrainepoem.com/. She is currently Murphy Visiting Fellow in Poetry at Hendrix College and lives in Little Rock, Arkansas with her two kids, cat, dog, and husband.

what's left

of my city? or better yet admit
that it was never mine
or yours or theirs or anyone's
yet tanks enter Crimea
flags go up bodies down
to knees but this is not
the city I was born to nor
its country where the river twines
lilac rimmed and twins
from Dnepr to Dnipro where
I followed the crunch of chestnuts
but now they've all been crushed by tanks
entering Crimea and the nation
of my birth does not exist
—if nation ever did—

what binds us then if not a kind
of language? a Slavic or slave
root? the cry for *Krim*? a crime?
or what came on too easily
as childhood speech? what binds us
if not this body? history of tanks
entering Crimea where memory is shaped
by news translated into foreign words
I've made my own incomprehensible
and kept unspoken tanks entering
Crimea and a poet—bourgeois wasp
without the sting—dedicates "a piece
to the Ukraine" not knowing its origin in
okraina | outskirt | border |edge | *na kotoroi* | on which
you stand | never in |never *v Ukrainye* | always *na*

and still I write in English with only
a Russian tongue of *na na na* a blood-song ringing
as tanks enter Crimea where my grandparents
spent summers watching the sun
set Soviet on the Black Sea telling my mother
fairytales of fish whose every golden scale could grant
a wish or turn into a body: child who breathes
beneath the waves without language | country | city | scape |
but water no home save one where tanks
become stray dogs that never learned
to swim and we know nothing
of Crimea and I know even less
of what is left

        previously published in *Springhouse Journal's Frogpondia*

An erasure of "Address by the President of the Russian Federation"
February 21, 2022
22:35, The Kremlin, Moscow

mir**in**
Ukraine

is

country

and after

a few

words   history

entirely created

by Russia

severing what is historical

Nobody asked

for   War

longed

for

distance

found

sh ine

Let me repeat

its people

not   a mistake

admit

them openly and honestly

12

                              Ukraine
                                        fully
                                                        Ukraine
            call
                        Ukraine

    Go   back to history   repeat
                                    it was impossible

                              any   future

                  instead
                                                bodies
            wonder : why

                                          remain

    Despite   injustice

      Ukraine
                                                declare

                        Ukraine
                                                respect
                                                Ukraine
            reach   Ukraine
                                          gold
                                                      rope
    Never

    Ukraine   open
                              Ukraine
                        bin d   this   dictator
                              striking   Ukraine

```
                                        Ukraine
                        I would
            men     d              memory

                    generations   Ukraine
            branches
    r           i v     er s
                                wave
                        burned

                                But we know

            Ukraine
            split           is

                        water

                                        air
                    Black Sea
            fracture
is

                                lack and lost

                                        in tatters

                                                Ukraine
        its
         root
                            carries on


                                    – listen carefully, please –

        previously published in *Rattle*'s Poets' Respond
```

January, 2014

Dear Birthplace,

In 1993, the USSR had already collapsed, I was already six-years old, and you were already a sovereign nation. Only then, after years trying to flee, my family was granted Jewish-refugee status and allowed to leave you, Ukraine, never to return or regret leaving.

I remember little of your then mostly Russian speaking Dnipro. My *Rodina,* birth-city, homeland I never knew as home. I recall the sausage and Kvass street-vendors we couldn't afford; the rusting fountains I walked when the river flooded; the hours in line, waiting for bread and eggs and milk and tomorrow; and the neighborhood boys, who once threw stones at me because I was a little *zhid* girl playing on their street. And this, I thought, this was trauma. And our final departure, that rain-drenched winter, a break from the language and world I was just learning to read, this was trauma too.

But today, when my American soil is covered by heavy-white, Soviet-like January snows, while Kyiv's streets are melting, rutted with fire and ash-tarred bodies, I know that I know nothing of your trauma.

When the police are shooting and beating and tearing into your own people on their own streets—brother's body against a brother's against their mother—I can't begin to know your unearthed demons, the death sinking into your once envied *chernozyom* with the hope of leaving roots.

Can't begin to understand what violence mutilates your body: a starving tree grown wild and violent: a cracking flesh that I believed was once my country.

And I close my eyes, try to think harder, to remember or imagine it, that ghost elusiveness of you. But I recall only the train ride to your capitol city, and the hardboiled eggs we pealed while playing cards on the top bunk. Too young to understand them then, the games, the very gamble we were taking.

We won. I know that only now. But I have lost the way to place the place of you, of motherland, inside my mind. I want to remember Kyiv's central square, Maidan, standing there before its fountains or seeing it shrink below through the window of an airplane, but nothing comes, and so I watch a recent video of a journalist hit with a grenade amidst the burning barricade and faceless military men. And that square, that you, is somewhere in the background, lost in all the smoke and panic: first aflame and then a grave.

I read the news, watch footage of "medieval violence," as one reporter called it, but feel only pressure. An iron lung, the weight of memory or its lack. The fear of losing people and a country.

> *Not mine, its someone else's wound*,
> Anna Akhmatova whispers.

And in writing myself into your story, I know I am at fault—an artful imbedding, a weed trying to thrive in an estranged history.

So instead, I'll go back to Caruth and Freud, and all their distant trauma theory. I'll watch their pages thin to legible skin, but turn meaningless in the face of what is real and indescribable. In the face of "the trauma" I thought I knew, the one I know I cannot touch. The too soon forgotten foreign bodies bleeding in your own Slavonic name. A country shattering like a red-gold teacup.

I try to carry it, this story. Try to write it across the Atlantic. But it is yours, and yours alone. I have no right to it. Mourning must be earned.

Forgive me, *Rodina*—ground where I was born. Forgive me, *rodnaya*—my dear, my native familial flesh. And I'll forgive that you are not a motherland who grants forgiveness.

> previously published in *Grist*

Lila Dlaboha was a 2018 finalist in the Marsh Hawk Press Poetry Prize judged by Jane Hirshfield. She was born of Ukrainian immigrants on the Lower East Side of Manhattan. She was recently short-listed for the Poetry International Prize 2021. Her poems have appeared in *Arts & Letters* (Georgia College), *Bellevue Literary Review*, *Mudfish*, Andre Codrescu's *Exquisite Corpse*, among other publications. On and off since 2016 she has been volunteering with children in the war zones of Ukraine.

Excerpts from My Notebook: Ukraine 2017

Punkt

Today I helped out at the Railroad Punkt in Kyiv, the place where soldiers meet to catch the military train that takes them to the front. They told me that they had to pay for the tickets themselves.

We gave them sandwiches, coffee or tea, sweets and fruits, and little talismans to wear or keep in their pockets—thumb-sized rag dolls with big boobs, braided blue-and-gold bracelets, or wooden crosses on a string that we tied around their necks.

Many soldiers wanted to talk with me when they learned that I was an American. They considered it a blessing of some kind, a good luck charm.

Kolya is an artillery gunner, father of two, from Chernihiv. Tonight he is very drunk and sweaty. His cheekbones look toasted, eyes hollowed, bloodshot, squished, his face blackened and blotched red.

"I've got a bad feeling about this tour," he told me. "'I've already done 14 months and they're mobilizing me again."

The anxiety in that waiting area gelled with intensity. It was mobbed with some 60 soldiers, some of them looking surprised, as if they were just punched, pacing the floor, watching *Rambo* or some other war movie.

It would take at least eight hours to get to the war zone. Plenty of time to have your life pass in front of you over and over.

I had to say something that would reassure these soldiers that they will come out of the war alive. That's what they wanted to hear, needed to hear, so that's what I gave them.

Very quickly, a line started to form in front of me:

"Tie the bracelet on me, it will keep me alive."
"Kiss me before I go it will keep me alive."
"Put your arms around me it will help me survive."

Avdiyivka

In 2016, Avdiyivka was devastated by missiles fired by Russian troops that had destroyed and occupied nearby Donetsk City.

There's no leftover food in Avdiyivka. Scraps are put out on the curb for animals that cower and look at you sideways, bones sticking out.

They sag and press to the ground with each tired step just like the people who still live here.

The apartment where I'm staying is right across fields that are littered with mines. As soon as I arrived I was told not to walk there.

The missionaries took me in, there was nowhere else to stay. They don't lock their door—this more than anything else surprised me.

One night when there was no shelling, we watched *Sound of Music* together, dubbed in Russian, four ladies eating popcorn stretched out on a queen-sized bed.

They borrowed the apartment from a family who had run away during the onslaught.

Luba is always thinking ahead. Chased and displaced people will do that.

"Today they may kill us," she told me, matter-of-factly. "I must be dressed well." Her cascading mane of bleach-blonde hair bounces around her shoulders.

Luba and the other missionary ladies make a point of dressing nicely every day so that the separatists can't call them bums when they're killed.

The Lake

The missionaries and I went on foot to the lake, a manmade lake, to unwind. It was a long walk from city center, across the railroad tracks into the rural area with single-family homes, cottages.

There were many people at the lake, women in bikinis, men in skimpy spandex, fat and slim, eating sprats in oil, drinking homemade vodka, Ukrainian pop music blaring from the snack bar, colorful umbrellas all along the sandy beach.

Nice place to go to in the middle of a war—if it wasn't for all the missiles flying from the east, landing behind the bulge at the edge of the lake.

Big sign says NO SWIMMING ALLOWED. Of course, people are swimming. They paid 10 hryvni at the gate, you can bet they're going to swim.

Suddenly: Loud sounds of BOOM BOOM every minute or so, and missiles whistling. No one flinched or even turned their head.

Some time passed, more and more whistles then BOOM, maybe one or two kilometers away, no more. Then black smoke rising from right behind the bulge.

Something was hit just beyond the lake, behind a little bump in the terrain.

I saw a woman I met earlier, at the high-school graduation I was invited to when I arrived. She sang so beautifully from her belly to serenade me, welcome me to Avdiyivka.

She and two girlfriends and her husband are on beach blankets laughing, eating sprats out of a can, sausage, bread, and drinking wine. I come over to say hello to them.

"Did you tell Trump hello from me?" She's a bit tipsy. She's been asking me that ever since we met.

Suddenly, [WHISTLING] then BOOM BOOM, black smoke. No big deal again, no one reacted. Again, the missile falls right behind the swell of land on the edge of the small lake.

Why do they keep shelling that same spot, over and over again? It occurred to me that Ukrainian troops must be entrenched there.

The separatists have been bombing this old section of Avdiyivka a lot, home of ordinary people, many old people. I think they want to take over this recreational area is why. They want it for themselves.

Everyone knows that lots of separatists live in Avdiyivka. They go back and forth to the front from here, it's walking distance.

They come home on the weekend then return to the front on Monday, or whenever they rotate, like a job. That's why they're not really shelling the center anymore—they're aiming for this rural area.

Kateryna

Kateryna is becoming a pain in the ass. I don't like her. I think she's following me. Calling me often, wants to meet. I don't trust her.

She's originally from Moscow but now lives in Barcelona, so she says, carries a camera with her all the time, she takes lousy pictures of me, claims to be a photographer.

I heard that one before from other people who were snooping into my business. I suspect she's been sent from Moscow to look in on me.

The shooting gets worse at the lake.

[WHISTLING], BOOM BOOM, more whistles then BOOM, again whistles, BOOM, BOOM. But we don't see them. We just hear them and see the black smoke behind the bulge. You could swim there, it's that close.

Now the people begin to panic, start collecting their things, blankets, they don't even bother dressing.

The missionaries were not in a hurry, though, said they still want to stay. The music in the food pavilion was playing loudly, the missionaries took it all in stride, confident no bomb was going to fall on the lake's disco. The so-called separatists will surely spare it for their own amusement.

Kateryna asked my acquaintances if there's room for two of us in their car. The three women, big ladies, and one husband, pile in, I sit on someone's lap.

Missiles flying. [WHISTLING], BOOM, black smoke. Everyone is talking at once, telling others what to do, what should be done, what not to do.

We're all squished and the husband starts the car and drives it straight into deep sand. The car sinks, stuck deep. More than half the wheel is buried in sand.

We all spill out of the car. We try to dig it out with our hands, doesn't work.

I call Semen. Kateryna for some reason is yelling at me not to call him, tries to grab my phone out of my hand. Says, "No!"

He is head of the *Simiky* here, civilian/military affairs, but frankly I don't think he does much of anything other than patrol the streets and beat up drunkards. I've taken strolls with him in the evening.

I tell him the situation. People are in a panic, the driver drove the car into deep sand, can't get out and they're shooting pretty heavily.

[WHISTLING], BOOM, black smoke. Perhaps you can come and help dig us out, help evacuate people out of here. This is your job, is it not?

He sighed loudly, a give-me-a-break kind of sigh.

What was I thinking? The *Simiky* are made up of former militia that was fired throughout Ukraine after then-president Yanukovych was kicked out. They just redeployed some of them to the war zone.

The missionaries walk over, perfectly calm, hook up the car with rope and pull us out of the sand.

My acquaintances dropped Kateryna off at a checkpoint because she is staying with the *Simiky* somewhere not in my direction. The *Simiky* didn't want to give me a place to stay, when I had asked them, interesting, but thank goodness. I was glad to be rid of her.

I come home to the missionaries' apartment and as usual the door is not locked. I was glad to see equanimous Luba whom everybody admires. She is the oldest of the missionaries here, but still much younger than me. I told her about the drama at the lake.

Suddenly, who walks into the apartment: Kateryna. She comes in with the missionary Natalia saying, "Don't worry, I'm only here to charge my phone and transfer some files." She could have gone home to do that, to the *Simiky*. I suspect she just wanted to see where I'm staying.

Now it really begins to look suspicious—her coming to Avdiyivka, finding me, weaseling her way into the apartment, making some excuse, always wanting to get together. It annoys me and she sees this.

Next Day

I've got the stiffest neck.
The fly in my room bothers me more than the sound of bombs.
There was supposed to be a ceasefire to collect crops.

BOO-BOOM
Pheeewwwww [WHISTLING]
Plaafff
Phaatt Phoedt Huhmphd
Thump pump pump pump pump

I'm sitting on my bed and listening
on a pivot of my whole anatomy
compelled to give form to sound
to each round of fire

What for? Why this obsession with sound as if I could snuff out the bombs if only I could fit them into my mouth.

The building shook—incoming.

Damn fly.

Day After

Bombs are falling as I hang the laundry out on the balcony three stories up.

I feel the floor shake. Incoming again.

When I flap the shirt I'm about to hang, I'm startled by the sound it creates, a kind of thump that's similar to the sound of a bomb hitting packed turf a couple kilometers away.

But here it's right inside my palm. I jolted from the sound of a bomb in my palm.

Returning from the Front

I'm riding back to Pokrovsk in a military ambulance, up front sits a tight-lipped commander. In back I'm next to a handsome medic who is wounded but not badly, so he told me.

I can't see the wound and he's not eager to talk about it, so I let it go. He has a nice full ruddy beard and glassy blue eyes. His call name is *Vovk*, Wolf. He may not even be a medic for all I know.

This time I want to sit on the stretcher in case they smoke and open the windows again, because the last time when I sat on the bench in the back the wind blew straight in my face.

I caught a bad cold that way, on the way over to Avdiyivka. And now an earache, I didn't want to make worse.

The stretcher was threadbare, metal parts protruding into my rear end. Wouldn't you know it, on the way back no one smoked, so the window remained closed.

I could've sat on a nice padded bench. The road to/from the front is all chewed up, I had to hold on tight or fall off my seat.

I looked down at my feet and see that I'm not wearing any socks. SHIT. I looked over at *Vovk* and said "I forgot my socks!"

Full of lament, I locked eyes with him, and suddenly we both burst out laughing, the absurdity of the regret, of leaving my socks at the front, as if socks even mattered. We both laughed so hard, who the hell cares about socks.

How perfect it really was to return from war with only your socks missing.

I wanted to kiss him and laugh, embrace him and kiss him and laugh—it would keep us alive.

Boris Dralyuk was born in Odesa in 1982 and immigrated to the United States in 1991. He is the editor-in-chief of the *Los Angeles Review of Books* and translator of Isaac Babel, Andrey Kurkov, Mikhail Zoshchenko, and other authors. His poems have appeared in *The New York Review of Books*, *The Hopkins Review*, *The New Criterion*, and elsewhere. His collection *My Hollywood and Other Poems* appeared from Paul Dry Books in 2022.

Pantoum of a Public Park

Felled patriarchs, deracinated, lame,
they plant themselves at parks on folding chairs
for Préférence — a hoary plain-trick game —
to pass the time, to whist and bid misère.

They plant themselves at parks on folding chairs,
who once could not have spared a daylit hour,
and pass the time, and whist or bid misère,
like spellbound warriors robbed of their power.

Who once could not have spared a daylit hour
now look intently at their idle hands
like spellbound warriors robbed of their power,
feeling the futile draw of distant lands.

Now look intently at their idle hands:
those muted throbs, those twitches they restrain
tell of the futile draw of distant lands,
of what they were, of what they must remain —

felled patriarchs, deracinated, lame.

Anna Frajlich was forced into exile by the government's anti-Semitic campaign in 1969, making her home in New York City, where she taught at Columbia University for over three decades and became one of the foremost poets writing in the Polish emigration. She has more than a dozen books of poetry in the original Polish to her credit, as well as five bilingual editions of her work (English, French, Italian, Spanish, Ukrainian). Frajlich received the Oscar Halecki Prize from the Polish American Historical Association for her book *The Ghost of Shakespeare: Collected Essays*, and has been awarded literary prizes from the Turzański Foundation and the Kośielski Foundation, among many others.

Ronald Meyer is the editor of Frajlich's *Ghost of Shakespeare: Collected Essays* (2021) and a special issue of *The Polish Review* devoted to Frajlich's work (March 2022). He is the translator of Anna Akhmatova's *My Half-Century: Selected Prose* and Dostoevsky's *The Gambler and Other Stories.* He is currently translating *The Laboratory,* Frajlich's collection of short prose. He teaches a seminar in Russian literary translation at Columbia University.

Flight from Lviv

Not since the death of my parents
have I heard so many times
the name of the city of
Lviv
from which one inevitably
had to flee in a hurry.

in 1914 my three-year-old father
and his parents
fled the pogrom to Prague
where for three years they lived
on imperial vouchers
before returning to Lviv.

the second war and the Russians

drove father to a camp in the Urals
my pregnant mother
ran away on foot
before catching the train
to Kirghizia

while those who remained in Lviv
met death on every street corner

on the television I see
mothers and children running to the station
the mothers shielding their children from the camera
as once again they flee from Lviv.

Born in Cleveland, Ohio, to postwar immigrant parents, **Luba Gawur** is a first-generation Ukrainian-American. Some of her English and Ukrainian-language poems have been published in *Terminus*, *Kubans'kyi Kurier*, and *Suchasnist' Casper Star Tribune*. In 2016, Crisis Chronicles Press published her collection of poetry, "Scraping the Sky" and Smoloskyp published her Ukrainian-language book, "The Tale About the Little House by the Little Woods."

Wormwood *pollen*

Пил – dust in Ukrainian   Пилок – pollen   Полин - wormwood Pollen – dust, fine powder Chornobyl – Black stalk
By the wormwood of the buzzing forests   Stalks of healing herbs proliferate   Pods of poisoned seeds irradiate   it's late it's late, it's late
And atoms pollinate...
Pollen wafting through the singed air going forth and multiplying here, there, and everywhere, sowing mushrooms in the clouds, mushrooms in their loamy, blackened shrouds.
Blade upon chlorophylling blade – scorched, there is no refuge, no shade... the air is torched...
Black weed, white weed   Black stalk, tainted seed, evil greed... Good earth,

Adam's birth… Green grasses glowing
Pollination growing…
Black weed, white seed…   Blooming
buds of dangling   isotopes strewn as
scarlet runes   across the pine forest
floor… sister-trees forevermore.
Queen Bee – zoom to the Zone, hurry and
see! O come thou and come ye quickly!
Mother Mary, Crown of the prairies -
Bless the weed and the wood,   caress the
seed…may it bear fruit   of the knowledge
of good…for
 far-flung winds have blown – flowers
sown – overgrown…   …Honey shall be
succulent   …
…Heaven sent.

January 31, 2020

Bob Holman is a poet most often connected with the oral tradition, spoken word, poetry slams and digital poetry. He created the part of Captain John Smith in Yara's *Capt. John Smith Goes to Ukraine* and performed in *1917-2017: Tychyna Zhadan & the Dogs* at La MaMa. He generated two award-winning PBS series, *The United States of Poetry*, and a documentary on endangered languages, *Language Matters.* His grandparents were from Kamenetz Podolsk. www.bobholman.com

War Haiku

That crow on that fence
Uncaringly particular looks up
Just as bomb hits

Ukraine wheatfields wave
Winds wind eternity over homelandscape
Burial mounds? Bomb craters?

Bless the broken tanks, O Lord
They provide a place to hide behind
O Lord, Let the keys be inside

Send Out a Text

Send out a text
Encrypted, but easily decrypted
Including Ґ ґ, Є є, Ї ї and I i (letters
Only in Ukrainian alphabet)
Say we will be leaving Mariupal
At first light
5:30 am
By such and such route.
Then sleep in.

Send out a text
Encrypted, but easily decrypted
Including Ґ ґ, Є є, Ї ї and I i
(letters only in Ukrainian alphabet)
Saying *Stuff your bazookas with dirty undies*
Causing backfire and shitstains everywhere

Send out long, difficult to translate, text
(Using lots of Ґ ґ, Є є, Ї ї and I i)
(Letters only in Ukrainian alphabet)
Going into great detail re: the etymology
Of the word "bazooka" which in fact
Was named after a novelty musical instrument
Invented, built, named and played by
30s US comedian Bob Burns, who wasn't really that funny.
The instrument consists of two pieces of stove pipe
That slid into each other, trombone-esquely,
With a funnel welded onto the inner pipe.
The "instrument" was "played" by sliding the pipes
Back and forth exuberantly while humming
Into the pipe opening. There was no mouthpiece,
Only a buzzing embouchure. So it was somewhat
Kazoo-like, a hint of how the name came to be.
By this time the Russian soldiers tasked
With translating this Trojan horse of a message
Will be falling asleep,
A perfect time to attack them.
With a bazooka, of course.

Poem for Oleh Lysheha (1949-2014)
on the Occasion of the Publication (Finally!) of your *Dream Bridge*
(Lost Horse Press, Contemporary Ukrainian Poetry Series Volume 10, Bilingual, Translated by Tkacz & Phipps)

Tonight was your book launch, Oleh!
We missed you
But, surprise,
The books were there!
In the Small Press Poetry World (actually,
Tiny Town), we know this to be a rarity.
It was a party,
Your friends were there, maybe a few enemies?
But we all made up and would have kissed
If it weren't for the damn COVID masks.
This being at the Ukrainian Museum on 6th St,
A stickler, as you know, for protocol (not your strong suit).
Maria, the Director, persisting still, even after two grinding years.
Ah well.
Julian's cousins have a band, Korinya. Violin, accordion
And what looked like a tenor (not bass) drum
With a single cymbal attached atop, played your stuff
Joyously, three young women singing through their
Foreheads in the Carpathian manner you loved so much.
Also, your poems which brought Nature right into the room,
As usual,
Animals and humans on equal footing. Pervasive
Undercurrent of spirituality, absolutely
No sanctimony, of course, *your* style. Virlana masterminded
The extravaganza, a parade of your poems in plays, film clips,
Live readings by Andrew and Sean and Olena and Wanda.
I read "Oak" and ending of my Intro to the book.
Julian on bandura, Paul on cello.
We hung out after, even Maria, drank all the wine,
And the crazy thing was, throughout
The whole night, not a single mention of the
War. The killing that was going on as we luxuriated
In your poetry and drank up all the wine
(Maybe a clue there?) eventually even removing

Masks (not everybody).
Katarina and her baby are now in Warsaw. Zhadan,
In Kharkiv, was going on a beer run
When a missile sliced right in front of his car.
Howitzer.
Try getting Howitzer into a poem. Try rhyming bandura with Howitzer.
As you were saying, a shot glass in the middle of the road, boiling
Eggs with a hammer. The bridges,
Bombed in retreat (this is still going on) (right now).
Pontoons (not in your poems), trying to get back across.
Trying to safely leave town.
Picked up by a man with a load of radishes.
Taken to the train station in Zaporizhzhia.
Hiding in an underground dugout.
You can't really call it a bunker. The door's been blown off.
No stash of food or water. A phone charger. A loose shingle
In the wind.
An air raid siren.

Eugene Hutz was born outside of Kyiv and is the front man for the internationally acclaimed Gypsy Punk band -- Gogol Bordello. He created the group in 1999 playing clubs in the East Village. It was at that time that he worked with Yara appearing in *Circle* and *Song Tree* at La MaMa Experimental Theatre and heading the Nova Nomada project together with Julian Kytasty & Virlana Tkacz. Over the years Gogol Bordello expanded into ever large venues and festivals. Hutz's live performances with the band are legendary and have also electrified audiences the Whitney, Tate Modern and the Venice Biennale. His recent concerts have been benefits for Ukraine.

Serhiy Zhadan was born in the Luhansk Region of Ukraine and educated in Kharkiv where he lives today. He is the author of twelve books of poetry. His prose works: *Voroshilovgrad, Mesopotamia* and *The Orphanage* were awarded the Angelus Central European Literature Award, the BBC Ukrainian Book of the Year Award, and the Brücke Berlin Prize. He is the front man for the band Zhadan & the Dogs and has collaborated with Yara Arts Group since 2002. Yale University Press published his selected poems as What We Live For/What We Die For translated by Virlana Tkacz and Wanda Phipps in 2019. He was awarded the 2022 EBRD Prize in Literature for his novel *The Orphanage*.

Forces of Victory
(Ukrainian by Serhiy Zhadan, English by Eugene Hutz)

Те, що залишиться навіки –
це наше небо і наші ріки,
це світлі тіні богородиць.
Ми залишились, щоб боротись.

Ми тут жили і виростали.
Високе сонце над містами.
Це нас тримає щохвилини
гаряче небо України.

Це наші діти і дороги.
Крило пташине перемоги.
Це ми освячені з тобою
її вогнями і любов'ю.

Коли здається щи більше не можу
То справді знаю що переможу
Так прокидаються напівдороги
Сили перемоги

Так прокидаються всередені
Сили перемоги

I can't go on, I will on (6 times)

Olena Jennings is the author of the poetry collection *Songs from an Apartment* (2017) and the chapbook *Memory Project* (2018.) Her poetry collection *The Age of Secrets* is forthcoming from Lost Horse Press in Fall 2022. Her novel *Temporary Shelter* was released in 2021 from Cervena Barva Press. Her translation from Ukrainian of Vasyl Makhno's collection *Paper Bridge* is forthcoming from Plamen Press. She is the founder and curator of the Poets of Queens reading series and press.

My Ukraine

In the church on Scott Street in Milwaukee,
the paint chipping
from the recently retouched stairs,
a set that daunted
the woman with the cane.

My grandfather sat in the back row,
so that he could gossip with friends.
My grandmother sat with hers,
a lace scarf over her head.
I felt alone, swooning from incense.

Sometimes I would go out in the backyard
where I liked to imagine the inside
of the apartment behind the church,
the rug that hung on the wall to keep
the room warm.

Now the chandeliers have gathered
a layer of dust.
Now there is a solitary bullet
hole in the midnight blue stained glass.
Now the walls are in danger of caving in.

We use our hands to hold them up,
news from Ukraine, an invasion.
We use our hands to hold up the trembling
walls. We won't let them
fall.

The voice of the choir resounds.
Keep Ukraine safe.

Menagerie

He held the cat
that his wife
had reflected in embroidery,
forming a face

in French knots,
the turning of the thread,
three times
father, son, and holy spirit.

The meow responded
in the rubble like a folk song,
words long forgotten,
a woman's lost voice in the air.

The neighbor, always in bare feet,
stepped like a saint over crumbled walls.
He said a prayer
over the body of an animal.

A bird flew by
and perched on the shards of a dish.
It was red, a beacon.

His feet bled,
leaving a trail
that led towards home.

Flying

Folded into the sky
like egg whites.
She is in her red jacket,
Climbing higher
in her swing.

The building has a gaping
hole and she will push
her way through.
She will see the people
below like dolls.

Grandpa is in the bedroom
watching black and white films.
Sister is the bathroom
washing her hair.
Brother is taking apart

a toy car, open
as their lives.
Suddenly their hearts
live
outside their chests.

Suddenly the bed
is torn in half.
Suddenly the tile
floor is full of rubble.
Suddenly the walls crumble.

When she reaches
the ground she peels
off her red coat
and walks away,
a refugee.

Ilya Kaminsky is the author of *Dancing in Odessa* (Tupelo Press) and *Deaf Republic* (Graywolf Press). His work was the finalist for the National Book Award and received The Los Angeles Times Book Prize. Originally from Odesa, Ukraine, he now lives in Atlanta.

What We Cannot Hear

They shove Sonya into the army jeep
one morning, one morning, one morning in May, one dime-bright morning—

they shove her
and she zigzags and turns and trips in silence

which is a soul's noise.
Sonya, who once said, *On the day of my arrest I will be playing piano.*

We watch four men
shove her—

and we think we see hundreds of old pianos forming a bridge from Arlemovsk to Tedna Street, and she

waits at each piano—
and what remains of her is

a puppet
that speaks with its fingers,

what remains of a puppet is this woman, what remains
of her (they took you, Sonya)—the voice we cannot hear—
is the clearest voice.

A Spell Against Bomb Makers

This, officers, is common chickweed,
cousin of a prickly sow thistle.

If you lean your ear
to her stem

you can hear
yourself leaving.

A Widower

Alfonso Barabinski stands in Central Square
without a shirt,
rakes up snow and throws it on
marching troops.

His mouth
drives the first syllable of his wife's name into Vasenka's walls—

He, on foot, a good mile and a half of wind,
sets off for the beach, on cobblestone streets, and stops every
woman he meets—

Alfonso Barabinski, vodka flask in his pocket, bites a hole in an
apple and in that hole
he pours a shot of vodka—
and he drinks *to our health*—
a toast to his wife shot in the center of town where her body

lies down.
Alfonso Barabinski, a child in his arms, spraypaints on the sea
wall PEOPLE LIVE HERE—

like an illiterate
signing a document
he does not understand.

Olga Livshin was raised in Odessa and Moscow, and came to San Diego as a Jewish refugee with her parents. Her poetry and translations appear in *Ploughshares, the Kenyon Review Online,* and *Modern Poetry in Translation*, among other journals, as well as anthologies including *Words for War: New Poetry from Ukraine.* She is the author of *A Life Replaced: Poems with Translations from Anna Akhmatova and Vladimir Gandelsman.*

Translating a Life

for O.M. and M.R.

Someone spread a blanket of wild buckwheat
over a meadow. Someone tucked puffball pillows
in each corner of the purple-green sheet.
It is summer everywhere, except war.
War, where it used to be home,
and now, war by government, here.
And what does it matter that the meadow
seduces the bees in pollen, or me in lines
of a poem, or that I hear perfectly good
Russian names for plants and translate them
into You-and-Me-ish? Take the tea mushroom,
the little fox mushrooms and piggies,
the early field-dweller, the mysterious
cheese-eater. These words are undocumented
here, and the country that sent them erases
every syllable with its crimes.
Take an under-birch-mushroom
anyway—it's a choice edible,
birch bolete in your tongue, on
the tongue. The language for falling in love
with forests, and stories, and friends
does not care who's killing whom.
Unfortunately, I care. And, sitting here
by a huge flowering bush, I see no refuge.
What languaged fantasy could stop us
from being murderous strangers? Would you
take a Russian mushroom name,
tuck it in your lapel for the brief banquet of life?
Does that translate anything else for you? Is this
how it works?

> previously published in *A Life Replaced: Poems with
> Translations from Anna Akhmatova and Vladimir Gandelsman*
> (Poets & Traitors Press, 2019)

Oksana Lutsyshyna is an award-winning writer, translator, and literary scholar. The latest of her poetry collections, *Persephone Blues*, was published in the English translation in 2019 by Arrowsmith. Her latest novel *Ivan and Phoebe* (2019) has been awarded the UNESCO Lviv City of Literature Award in 2020, and Shevchenko National Prize (2021). Oksana Lutsyshyna is currently a Lecturer in Ukrainian Studies at the University of Texas at Austin.

***

ось так чується місто під облогою -
середина його найсерединнішої площі
болить мов обпечена
ніби цілими днями хтось хлюпає і хлюпає окропом або смолою
бо ворожі війська надто далеко а окріп надто близько
і не можна залишати його на завтра

ось так виють його собаки і скаженіють у стійлах його коні
ось так відчувають повний місяць і не можуть вирватися до нього
ось так виють усі хором - що там святий Августин казав про дихання?

ось так його стіни здригаються наче хвилі
наче хвилі в океані із дна якого вибухає вулкан
і як хвилі ці стіни відступають і наступають
як хвилі, як вороги, даруючи гнів і надію

як довго це місто ще простоїть? місяць каже -
ну, а якщо вічність? якщо не стане краще, якщо все
триватиме і триватиме - опіки, хвилі, що там
іще буває у містах під облогою? витримаєш?

і ти видихаєш і кажеш, твердо дивлячись йому в єдине око:

витримаю

***

нічого не стається нічого не стається
все підвисло як Шульцівська ніч липнева
може це ретроградний меркурій
але чому чорт ціле життя виглядає як
суцільний ретроградний меркурій?..
чому там немає інших планет
крім цього меркурія?...

ніхто не приходить ніщо не приходить
навіть бісова пошта не приходить
приходять тільки якісь купони на піцу

ну в принципі це покращення
бодай не на оцет із радянського магазину

біля церков колись ставили камені
великі брили
для тих хто мусив виплакатися і не знав де
або не знав як
камінь кликав їх до себе кам'яним голосом

казав - я буду серцем твого літа

серцем липневої ночі

***

живи кажуть тут
не можу - забагато спогадів
тоді тут
не можу - тут все чуже
тут жоден спогад не приживеться
де ж тоді житимеш?
є така книга
ти сама її написала
і там, у її дощах, тобі найтривкіше
і десь там у її джунглях ти заблукала
пальми її і квіти
дикі її бугенвілії
її каламутні ріки
десь там ти сидиш над водою
у клітці з повітря

Kristina Lucenko teaches writing and rhetoric at Stony Brook University. She has translated into English the work of Ukrainian poet Vasyl Makhno, and written reviews of theatre and poetry, including Yara Arts Group performances and Serhiy Zhadan's *What We Live For, What We Die For.*

What We Dream

When he was a boy my father practiced it again and again,
wanting to perfect his new American signature.
Ls swoop like unfinished eights wandering off
at the *o*, a studied carelessness, a practiced future.

Some little things if you do them
long enough amount to big things.

At least this is what he taught me. He taught me that
yes, warriors are clever in everything. But strong doesn't mean big.
And the struggle doesn't stop at your door.

He taught me that melodies, lyrics, whole songs
won't be forgotten if we sing them in waking and sleeping hours.
Do you hear it, when your eyes are closed, your heart's beating
history?

And so in the dream I listen to your voice,
your voice is like a holding place.
We sing and wait for the clouds to gather,
and we measure time

not by anger or sadness or fear but by the sublime
and defiant tune rising,
a repertoire we have always known, of course,
a river flowing, flowing,
a nation inside us rising vast and wild like the moon.

Stash Luczkiw was born in New York City. He's the author of 3 recent books of poetry: *Inlays*, *Selah* and *Vineworks*. He works as a translator and has just completed a soon to be published novel set against the war in Ukraine called *Ashen Glory*. He currently lives in Italy.

Rage

We scroll through salvos
of grim information.
We watch the images
till our temples hurt.
We listen to the curses
meant to make sure we know.
And with each scream
our stiff fingers itch
to pull some trigger
that might lift us up
from years of indifference,
might slip us across the border
between slack-jawed paralysis
and righteous rage.
So we witness: how they wail
to move us into action,
while we wither in doubt
or exult in our anger,
aspiring to a glorious wrath.
Because we are human,
and being so human we desire
to be free—so free
we can fight off the fury
consuming us, fight
with still deeper ire.

Black Earth

The earth over here
is black—as black
as the world's first mother.
And I am her son.
She feeds me her dances
and dirges at dawn.
At night she watches
my bonds come undone
and fills me with longing
to scour her skin.

The earth over here
will soon be cratered, like faces
disfigured beyond recognition,
shellshocked and haunted
by glory's silent shadows:
seething men and lip-bitten women
eager to mete out revenge.

The earth over here
is wet—as wet as a fresh
orphan's face at the sound
of a strange woman's voice.
And I fear—for the child,
like a child unable to explain
how we can cease to exist.

The earth over here, it runs
with us—as it's run with blood
from the world's first plow—
and will keep running
toward the dire glow at the end
of the road to that limitless steppe.

Valya Dudycz Lupescu has been making magic with words (and food) for more than 20 years, incorporating folklore from her Ukrainian heritage with practices that honor the Earth. Valya earned her MFA in Writing from the School of the Art Institute of Chicago. Her work has appeared in *The Year's Best Dark Fantasy & Horror, Kenyon Review, Gargoyle Magazine, Strange Horizons, Mythic Delirium,* and others. Valya is the author of *The Silence of Trees*, and co-author of *Forking Good: An Unofficial Cookbook for Fans of The Good Place* and *Geek Parenting*. Valya's graphic novel, *Mother Christmas,* is forthcoming from Rosarium Publishing in 2022. You can read more on her website: www.vdlupescu.com or on Twitter: @valya

Ми тут (We are here)

We learned to live in translation,
raised with the restless understanding
that we come from ghosts
you have to believe in
to see.
If we did not stain our fingers red from beets for borshch,
knock on wood, learn to layer wax and paint on raw eggs,
and never whistle in the house,
if we did not memorize and chant,
trade Saturday morning cartoons
for lessons about Shevchenko, Stalin, and the Holodomor—
we might disappear.
And now, today,
because "Ukrainian" would not fade away,
culture not replaced, language not erased,
again they try to make us invisible,
borders redrawn with body bags,
and every mother's heart a bomb.

    Previously published in *Rust and Moth*

This poem is not enough

still it reaches places I cannot,
shines a light on neat and polished
fingers on phones,
buttons ready to launch a block
buster from the audience.
Polite flag-waving, hashtag-spreading
suits and skirts applauding
in fine shoes and finer postures
to participate...this massacre will be televised.

What wonderful warriors!
Such bravery! Such passion!
Blood less red than games of squids or thrones,
less glamorous their gashes and broken bones.
Their children cry a tad too loud,
and old babas with their sighs and signs,
sunflowers and shaking fists
a little heavy-handed,
but overall a fine spectacle,
inspiring and so important
until it isn't.

100 days and still the fire falls from the sky,
and lions look for the next bite.
The sacrifice is not enough,
a superbowl of bombs and borders,
story of freedom broadcast
from a safe distance.
In the trenches, one president refuses
to run, repeats his people's cry for help
as "never again" becomes conditional.
On the high ground of good intentions,
another president calls to his court:
"Stand and send
an unmistakable signal
to the world and Ukraine."
And they did.
The signal is not enough.

Sviat Vechir (Holy Night)

Parania, my Baba, dough dried on round, wrinkled cheeks,
creates the world in her kitchen.

She whispers well-kneaded wishes over beeswax candles
to saints watching like neighbors from icons on the wall.

Each of the twelve overflowing bowls a promise
carried across countries, tucked away in hems and fists.

"Who will see the first star?" she says,
a challenge not a question.

My cousins settle into stillness at the front room window,
listening for carolers, watching for the prize.

I stay behind, invisible in coke-bottle glasses and ten-cent Tolkien,
watching the magic of wheat and beets become communion,

Baba's hands holy, her songs a prayer,
the kitchen filled with grateful ghosts.

Vasyl Makhno is a Ukrainian poet, prose writer, essayist, and translator. He is the author of fourteen collections of poetry and most recently the book of poems *One Sail House* (2021). His poetry collection *Paper Bridge*, translated by Olena Jennings, is forthcoming from Plamen Press. He has also published a book of short stories, *The House in Baiting Hollow* (2015), a novel, *The Eternal Calendar* (2019), and four books of essays, *The Gertrude Stein Memorial Cultural and Recreation Park* (2006), *Horn of Plenty* (2011), *Suburbs and Borderland* (2019), and *Biking along the Ocean* (2020). Makhno's works have been widely translated into many languages; his books have been published in Germany, Israel, Poland, Romania, Serbia and the US. Two poetry collections, *Thread and Other New York Poems* (2009) and *Winter Letters* (2011), were published in English translation. He is the recipient of Kovaliv Fund Prize (2008), Serbia's International *Povele Morave* Prize in Poetry (2013), the BBC Book of the Year Award (2015), and Ukrainian-Jewish Literary Prize "Encounter" (2020). Makhno currently lives with his family in New York City.

Читання в Нью-Джерзі

Я приїхав читати в іржаве Нью-Джерзі
слухачі товклись біля входу у черзі
гомоніли – чекали поки їх впустять
у програмі – вірші та концерт піаніста
вперше заїхав до цього міста
дивно – на вулицях майже пусто

ґелґотіли у залі й шипіли зі струмом
на якому провисли повітря струни
всідались присутні – рипіли стільці
це читання відбулось в міському театрі
що ж цьому містові прочитати
і що ж прочитати їхній ріці?

коли перший голос доторкнувсь мікрофона
коли в дріт увійшла верліброва форма
дехто з публіки їв – дехто пив чай
але зала не стала одним радаром чи вухом
й поетів майже ніхто не слухав
і кожен стояв самотній як каланча

це було випадкове збирання коштів
дехто прийшов із дому – дехто із пошти
дехто з дітьми з недільної школи
прийшли як приходять на рок-концерти
або ж на недільну месу до церкви
всівшись наче кульбабки півколом

я сидів на тому читанні в Нью-Джерзі
наче річка тримала мене при березі
берег молочний туманом прикритий
верещали діти й гасали по залі:
до поезії в них не було найменшого жалю
до поетів – тим паче жодної крихти

і коли для читання підійшла моя черга
я простояв хвилину перед ними чемно
і сказав що потрібно послухати тишу

що слова потребують вух та осмислень
що сполука поезії з киснем
синім спиртом пече і дише

і примовкли усі хоча діти казились
але потім й вони вибились з сили
і притихли як мовкнуть річки в дощі
я почав із «Війни» – тобто із обстрілів
що пощикують наче в трамваях компостери
й битим склом скрегочать вночі

я сказав що в країні моїй їх ровесники
загубили втікаючи капчики й мештики
і сидять по підвалах вибившись з сну
їхні очі прозорі як води Світязя
в них далекі вогні прибережні світяться
й сині риби гребуть плавниками по дну

я сказав: ні про що мені не розходиться
кожен вірш та від чогось собі народиться
кожна квітка тримається на стеблі
і тонкий голосок на цілу Україну
підставляє плече тій червоній калині
і як може підносить її від землі

я був вдячний за це провінційне Нью-Джерзі
за портові світла над водою промерзлі
за бешкетників в залі та їхніх батьків –
що тримається світ на воді і поезії
на кульбабі троянді бузку і гортензії
поміж світлом і темінню двох берегів

Ранішнє туркотіння горлиць

туркотіли горлиці нині – вже
річка буде звиватись вужем
будуть жовтіти родини кульбаб
над ранок почувся горличий спів
не було уночі для мене снів:
тільки дощ віді вчора кульгав

може для того щоб я почув
як трикутний дах – ґонтовий чуб
бився об дощ як пара крил
а може тому аби горличий світ
розповів мені про бузковий цвіт
і що все в них і нас із крихт

це вони сповістили мені про клейке
тріскання цвіту – таке стійке
повторення в космосі – й на вербі
волохатий пушок яким вона б'є
коли смерть із життям одночасно стає
містом з пагорбом на горбі

я подумав про річку яка горілиць
годуватиме пару моїх горилиць
Благовіщення – потім Страстний
тиждень – потім тіло повстане із
світла слова із мільярдів звізд
яких вигнав господар напастись

я подумав що курячій сліпоті
що підважила ґрунт по своїй простоті
що чекала на спів та дозвіл
перейде у спадок весняний дощ
її корінь проріс в чорноземний товщ
її цвіт румиґатимуть кози

я подумав про грицики й про кульбаб
і про «Страсті» які допише Бах
починаючи їх від Матфея

як цю музику влиту ув жили рослин
ми почуємо вухом разом із ним
зрівноважаться тенор і флейта

я подумав що горлиці – але ж Бах
розпустив свій хор – і та юрба
туркотіння туркоту туркотінь
розлетілася звуками зеленців
і над ранок почувся горличий спів
і кульгавий крок в дощовій воді

я почув що горлиці принесли
сім зернят винограду – як ті посли
нотний стан «Страстей» – весняну повінь
і оновлення те що чекає нас
їде їде панна весна
а над нею горлиці як над полем

Псальма Бучі

ми тепер їх уже не покличемо
ні питальним знаком – ні кличною
формою – яка у нас є
в кого руки заламано й скручено
хто лежить по вулицях Бучі
по дворах під дощем гниє

припильнує їх чорний ворон
чорним оком чорний як ворог
чи пригорне їх херувим
най мій вірш буде їм псальмою
за Андрієм Петром Оксаною
солоспівом і хоровим

най пропущені мною сполучники
вам полегшать побачити Бучу
і почути тривожний дзвін
херувим в камуфляжній формі:
най покаже стовпи і опори
і пробиті зазубрини стін

най згадає усіх поіменно
у цій псальмі кожен іменник
як присипаний глиною світ
хто ще дихав учора під соснами
хто дивився ув очі псові
при серпневім падінні звізд

я не знаю якою ж печальною
мусить бути печаль моя з псальмою
і яких ще потрібно слів?
Буча скручена скотчем й розстріляна
звірина із якою зустрілись ми
в десять рогів та сім голів

перед тими страстями і Страсною
седимицею ми із Тарасом...
над Андрієм Петром Оксаною

що пливуть по небу ридванами
і гучними – як дзвін - риданнями

поклонімося Бучі псальмою

Oksana Maksymchuk is a bilingual Ukrainian American poet, scholar, and literary translator. In the Ukrainian, she is the author of poetry collections *Xenia* and *Lovy* and a recipient of Ihor-Bohdan Antonych and Smoloskyp prizes. With Max Rosochinsky, she co-edited *Words for War: New Poems from Ukraine* and co-translated *Apricots of Donbas* by Lyuba Yakimchuk and *The Voices of Babyn Yar* by Marianna Kiyanovska. Oksana holds a PhD in philosophy from Northwestern University.

Siberian Transit

Freight cars, barely any stops. Rising
stench. Some say,
We'll get shot in the woods.
Others say, They'll waste us away
building dams, roads.
Nobody knows.

It's all happening
now & now—a shard
of my mother's soul
throbbing inside my throat.

As she speaks, she hands me a shot glass,
the convex meniscus of moonshine
shuddering with the train's
clickety-clack.

Me, I say, I too got a dowry:
strangers with kids
lined up by the track. *Maybe
they're getting extra rations
for the winter*, I think
in my mother's place. Never looking them
in the eye, I feign—and don't feign—
indifference.

We drink until it gets light outside
and the trees in the window frame read
like lines
from a poem in a language
waiting to be revived.

In the narrow corridor, I squeeze past
men in uniforms, brush shoulders with
refugees, clutching at
passport & cash stuffed inside
my pants, as a Rom with a soiled sack
gives me a sidelong glance.

*What are we to each other but a chance
at a rhyme* jingles a line
in my ear, as I lean over the toilet
throwing up.

      previously published in *The Cincinnati Review*

The Hunger of the Famished

Grandma floats
over the stovetop—
a cloud of light
Edges of her soiled robe
skim the kitchen floors

I sit by her side
small like a child
I'm all mouth—
the rest of the body
an afterthought

Please forgive me for always
thinking about food
Jittery jewels of meat jelly
laced with fat, jam-topped pancakes
blossoming out

From you I've learned how to
reuse matches, divide
a cake, and grow
another body
inside my own

In your tiny home
I devour all
I'm served, the third eye
of my belly button
seeing what you see

stacks of limbs
thin as firewood
on the side of the street
as your mother's hand
shields your eyes

To this day
a stash of rice
underneath a floorboard
In your drawer, like a memento,
a piece of bread

    previously published in *The Cincinnati Review*

The Art of Mnemonics

when the dust had settled, she began her search
she pushed her way through the rubble, stepping
over remainders of walls, climbing through
window holes, her body
choosing a path for itself, as if in a dream

she remembered the desk
her sister sat at in class, the stool
on which her mother perched herself
with a small crackling radio in her lap
her father's prayer rug

she wanted to see their places
empty, to learn that they were safe
somewhere else

she imagined
secret doors opening up on walls
like lips, angels
leading them out

That week I lost
my color vision and my sense of smell
All food tasted the same

I recovered them
bit by bit
over the years

Did you find them, I ask

Their shoes, yes
I remember pulling them off one by one

Pulling them out...
she corrects herself, looking away

        previously published in *Tar River Poetry*

Askold Melnyczuk's book of stories, *The Man Who Would Not Bow,* appeared in 2021. His four novels have variously been named a New York Times Notable, an LA Times Best Books of the Year, and an Editor's Choice by the American Library Association's *Booklist.* He is also co-editor of <u>*From Three Worlds*</u>, an anthology of Ukrainian Writers. His published translations include work by Oksana Zabuzhko, Marjana Savka, Bohdan Boychuk, and Ivan Drach.

The Sunday Before Easter

>*Dreadful it is*
>*How here and there*
>*Endlessly God disperses*
>*Whatever lives.*
>   Holderlin

1

I prayed each twilight with the crickets
as a boy to another boy, rapt
in his mother's blue-gowned arms:

Otche Nash.

Concentration is prayer;
Poetry the private psalm.

Sunday before Easter
before dawn revives
the city with its debonair
starlings, startled by weather

to wooing, behind
my desk, from where
in the window I can see your double
I pray the only way I can.

I tell my stories
because they are mysteries,

2

because
the little god who dwells within,
reflecting God, creating
worlds with names, remembers.

My country, formerly the sun
became the oil-slicked water;
sapped pine barrens and barren
suburbia;

the "Venice of New Jersey"
since it flooded every year;
at times, mountains
and ignitable, polluted air

feel familiar
as the silk of your bed,

the blue-gold silk of your breasts.

3

Lviv, Peremyshl, Berchtesgaden:
there God flared in
his latest conflagration, disguised
in brown, or agonized
green;

booted, buckled,
moustache trim, chin
shaved clean as an apple,

proud of himself,
his shining discipline,
the moral courage to shelve
tobacco, moonlight, women.

He puffed himself especially
on his talent for division,
like that evolutionary
wonder, the amoeba;

for rising early, spitting
in his own glum sun,
showering in splinters
of ice-water without wincing,

marching in unison
with himself, raising legs
muscled as if modeled on Rodin.
And he was proud
of his spired libraries

outstripping Alexandria

where the dead speak and the living are silent.

He often visited museum
ransomed by lions,
accompanied by an interpreter
from the far city of Babel.

God torched houses.
He castrated boys, inspired
women burning for food
to murder their husbands.

He turned his people back to light.
I saw none of this,

and remember.

4

These fairy tales mother
Lent me for lullabies.
What once delivered me to sleep
now keeps me up

long after the emaciated hands
of the clock unclasp
and splay to quarter-cross
and the cat, and you, sleep.

I tell you because
I come from a country
Which refuses to die

And my name will not give me away.

5

Because it happens again
at a different address:
the Lord himself lashes
himself.

>   previously published in *Poetry*

Nina Murray is a Ukrainian-born American poet and translator. Her translations from the Ukrainian include Lesia Ukrainka's *Cassandra* (HURI, 2022) and Oksana Zabuzhko's *Museum of Abandoned Secrets* (Amazon Crossing, 2011). Her most recent book of poetry is *Minor Heresies* (THR Press, 2020).

World Egg, Яйце-Райце

on an egg
lines run convex
become circles
кола
the patterns—bands
crosshatched like a freshly laid hedge

риби дерева
the stars and the bones underground
wrapped—
a dressing
бинт
an armor

inside
some say it is Paradise
золоторунні отари
golden-horned oxen
all manner of ripening crop
врожай abundance

but if it cracks open
who can herd all the sheep?
who will yoke those oxen?
загнуздає золотогривого огиря
that comes thundering out?
хто сховається від стоокого
who can hide
from the gold-eyed wolf?

better to keep the concave world
whole
put bands on it
let the Eden—*наш рай*—inside
graze and hunt undisturbed

take it out
hold it
during a thunderstorm
візьми
приклади до вуха

in the dead of the night
you'll hear the oxen low

how to write a poem for Bucha

have the kettle on behind you on a video call. steep the words its rattle and hiss grind up to make a cup tea. let it sit. soak a piece of knitting in it, rib by rib. now put the wool over your eyes and wait until it sucks out of them the sight of dogs shot dead in the street. wring it. dip daffodils in the resulting ink. wait for a storm. what's left on the petals, rain-torn, will be the poem.

I

say the three partitions of Poland
is an odd choice for dinner conversation
but when we moved
next to the crown of brick on a hill
the mortared memory of the Hapsburg empire
we sneaked into abandoned casemates
searched the slivered brickwork
for scratched clues
read of the cannons that fired
at the Bolshevik cavalry on its way to take Warsaw
and found
a draft-horse shoe
a hill always has
a history of possession
into its lineage
I was adopted

II

and what
was I given to keep?
the smells
      chocolate coffee
      excarnated chestnuts under our feet
      the whiff
      of burnt hide from the meatpacking plant
      red brick
      cow heads in the gables
      naves that portion out coolness in the summer
      like eucharist
      dreams
      of street car lines
      that go unfamiliar places
      abandoned bomb shelters
      dog shit on the sidewalks
      human behind every garage wall
      and a row of trees
my misericordia these
ghosts hum in the forests
oil the machines guns they buried
come calling
the list of your grandparents' sins

how can you write poems about mothers at a time like this

succor the mother in her time zone
the war zone
her exclusion zone—
you then have to explain
who drew it
admit you built it
your own
bubble
a cask
a karst in the ozone
inside it
she bends the walls
time has stopped—something about the way
she keeps count—
she makes it all "now"
everything nothing
but this
sometimes a utility bill

she curdles bullets
cans thistles and myrrh
she only feels self-fulfilled
when she is a prophecy
the cause and effect
the looped newsreel

Krystia Nora is a second-generation Ukrainian American who teaches writing and rhetoric at the Milwaukee Area Technical College. She has a PhD in Composition and TESOL from Indiana University of Pennsylvania. She also has a Bachelor of Music degree from Dana School of Music, inspired by her grandmother and great-grandmother who sang in the L'viv Opera. Her creative publications include the classical vocal CD *Ukrainian Dreams* with pianist Roman Rudnitsky, violinist Bohdan Subchak, and cellist Vit Fiala. She began her writing life with the essay "A Ukrainian Sunset" in the magazine *Our Life/Наше Життя* and recently started writing poetry, publishing in *Voices from the Attic, Volume XXVII* and *The Milwaukee Independent*.

As Russia invades Ukraine   I breathe

*

out
*

I felt this moment coming in my bones
inevitable   but hope for a free
future clouded my pessimism as
I forgot shared nightmares ingrained within
whatever languages we speak   now we
remember this   the ground says blood pollutes
joy   and cries echo after centuries
wind-carried across steppes   oceans   deserts
to our doorsteps   wherever we live   war
changes our equations so martyrs are
buried sloppily with their murderers
scattered seeds reverberate with sorrow
now the world resonates with our pain   hope
coexists with harsh melodies   dread songs

*
in
*

Great-aunt Xenia painted vased flowers
like Van Gogh   but more meaningful to me
because she made them   her Ukrainian
village churches flank my dining room walls
her grey cat curls over my Balinese
sleeping with breaths a century apart
I can feel her presence as we eat   sleep
even when I sing   her mother looks down
counts my rhythm   guides the house melodies
next to my grandmother who looks wistful
even before she lost her beloved
Lviv   mother   sister   as cold and hot wars
relegated love to letters and this
art found carefully wrapped in a closet

*
out
*

Happiness can be enjoying a child's
birthday party remembering fonder
pandemic times when we merely worried
about the virus   returning children
to Ukrainian school   restarting our lives
it's ignoring the texts from another
friend who wants to vomit after seeing
photos of Bucha   news I'd missed because
my girl was scared after a year apart
from her classmate   worried she'd be alone
but she's the last to regretfully leave
I pray my worries are as unfounded
that the Russians pulling back is not
the breath before bellowing fire and ash

*

in
*

As the war continues   I work to breathe
in sonnets before sleep   somnambulant
words settle across my screen   inspire me
to stroll further into shadowed paths   push
poems   music   myself out of my soul
into the spaces rippling around me
away into the dark breezes blowing
between us   I forget to be careful
of edges like my mom taught me to be
screened and shuttered   how far can we grow past
ourselves   each other   our homelands   shared blood
debts we carry to beloved left there
and those with us   of us   how much can be
pruned and remain whole   I am uncertain

*

out
*

Feeling deeply's a curse   especially
on a day when I struggled to read through
a Mariupol diary   then learn
my cousin's friend died fighting for Ukraine
I fumbled as we talked orthodoxy
should have placed my ears closer and listened
nightmares pile into pyres   absorb the air
in my blood   but I keep empathizing
an addict texted her American
child that she'd died   needs funeral money
to score the fix to make it true   can one
un/see dead   un/hear bombs   un/feel pain   yet
I don't blame God   love and light   incarnate
freedom   evil lives when we turn away

Dzvinia Orlowsky is a Pushcart prize poet, translator, and a founding editor of Four Way Books. She's published six poetry collections including *Convertible Night, Flurry of Stones*, winner of a Sheila Motton Book Award; and *Bad Harvest*, a 2019 Massachusetts Book Awards "Must Read" in Poetry. Her poem sequence "The (Dis)Enchanted Desna" was selected by Robert Pinsky as a 2019 winner of the New England Poetry Club Samuel Washington Allen Prize; and her and Ali Kinsella's co-translation from the Ukrainian of Natalka Bilotserkivets's poem sequence "Allergy" was awarded the NEPC Diana Der Hovanessian Prize. Dzvinia and Ali's co-translations of Bilotserkivets's poems, *Eccentric Days of Hope and Sorrow*, was published by Lost Horse Press in 2021 and short-listed for the 2022 International Griffin Poetry Prize.

Natalka Bilotserkivets's work, known for lyricism and the quiet power of despair, became hallmarks of Ukraine's literary life of the 1980s. The collections *Allergy* (1999) and *Central Hotel* (2004) were the winners of Book of the Year contests in 2000 and 2004 respectively. In the West, she's mostly known on the strength of a handful of widely translated poems, while the better part of her oeuvre remains unknown. Her poem, "We'll Not Die in Paris," became the hymn of the post-Chornobyl generation of young Ukrainians that helped topple the Soviet Union. She lives and works in Kyiv.

Ali Kinsella has been translating from Ukrainian for ten years. Her published works include essays, poetry, monographs, and subtitles to films. She holds an MA from Columbia University, where she wrote a thesis on the intersection of feminism and nationalism in small states. *Eccentric Days of Hope and Sorrow: Selected Poems by Natalka Bilotserkivets*, a collection she co-translated with Dzvinia Orlowsky from Ukrainian was published by Lost Horse Press in 2021. Her latest work, *Love in Defiance of Pain: Ukrainian Stories*, an anthology in support of Ukrainians today, is soon available from Deep Vellum Press. A former Peace Corps volunteer, Ali lived in Ukraine for nearly five years. She is currently in Chicago, where she also sometimes works as a baker.

Bridge
By Natalka Bilotserkivets
Translated by Ali Kinsella and Dzvinia Orlowsky

The air is as still and hot
as my body. Arched like a bridge
over a river. It's so quiet—the nightingales
must be drinking their own black alcohol.

No sounds. Only color and shades
spread out across the water.
Face up—that's how it was with me.
Evenings as glorious as spirits!

There are memory catastrophes.
They collapse into signs, halftones, details
of blocks, construction of rail,
inflows of blood, formulas for love.

I don't remember the color of eyes,
but their expression's still here—
when a devastating pulse of extreme temperature
drops from above onto the bridge.

> Reprinted from *Eccentric Days of Hope and Sorrow: Poems by Natalka Bilotserkivets*, translated from the Ukrainian by Ali Kinsella and Dzvinia Orlowsky (Lost Horse Press, 2021). With permission from Lost Horse Press.

November
> *after Natalka Bilotserkivets*

I turn the key, enter my room—
dark corners welcome me.
Muddy taste of rain,
leaves taken into hands,
I could throw my life away
And it'd scarcely make a sound...
Shall I go there, where tiles
of light lie in the fields,
to the cobweb's maze,
blood-illuminated words,
to where a stranger removes his gloves,
traces his finger from vein to heart?
Water revives with early snows,
washes fat roots beneath
sidewalks. Uncertain knock,
the glass lamp lit,
I could choke on light
that has yet to pass.

> Reprinted from *Except for One Obscene Brushstroke*, 2003, with permission from Carnegie Mellon University Press.

Elegy
> *For Ed Hogan*

Black tree shadows along the paved road
are a safe lake

intertwined with light, a rustling
of leaves undressing,

eager for winter, the cold they won't feel,
anticipating ground.

I'm going nowhere in particular today.
I'm three o'clock passing onto four,

among others whose hearts pump anonymously
at their own doorways, that swell

with excitement, occasional adventure—
packed knife, the apple forgotten.

I was nowhere, last night, in particular,
breathing in my room, dreaming of you—

taking off your jacket, untying your shoes, for you—
making you lighter,

pushing back the water. Today
leaves, scattered from trees,

fall from autumn skies—
from four o'clock passing onto five,

from anything meant to hold or save us.

> Reprinted from *Except for One Obscene Brushstroke*, 2003,
> with permission from Carnegie Mellon University Press.

Hope Was a Thing with Pink Feathers: Oksana Baiul

Hope was a thing with pink feathers
circling Olympic ice.
Despite her tender years,
a woman of great composure.

Circling Olympic ice for gold,
Ukraine! We could hardly believe our ears:
This woman of great composure,
 triple Lutz-flip-loop world premiere.

Ukraine! (We could hardly believe our ears)
representing the once orphaned and lost...
With a triple Lutz-flip-loop world premiere,
How much could one girl cost?

Representing the once orphaned and lost,
a dash of Broadway thrown in for good cheer.
How much could one girl cost?
Kerrigan, steely—no fame fetters yet or fear.

A little Broadway never hurt a routine—
Then: gold! Oksana cried and cried and cried.
Kerrigan gauged her steely dream:
It's taking twenty minutes for officials to find...

Oksana cried and cried and cried—let's say, triple-cried.
Post Soviet tears no longer held to ransom.
It took twenty minutes for Olympic officials to find
Ukraine's national anthem.

As Nancy Kerrigan's eyes demanded ransom,
her Vera Wang swan about to be pronounced dead,
still no copy of Ukraine's national anthem—
maybe they'd play Russia's instead.

No flowers, swans or poppies red,
at home, we held our breath.
Maybe they'd fly Russia's eagle instead.
But damn, this gold was our destined wealth.

At home, we waited, held our breath.
Where was our anthem, the homeland tether?
Slava Boha..! this could be our wealth.
Our hope was a thing with pink feathers.

>Reprinted from *Bad Harvest*, 2018, with permission from Carnegie Mellon University Press.

Maria G. Rewakowicz is a poet, translator and literary scholar. She holds a Ph.D. in Slavic Languages and Literatures from the University of Toronto and has taught Ukrainian literature at a number of universities, most recently at Rutgers University—New Brunswick, NJ. She has authored four collections of poetry in Ukrainian and two monographs of literary criticism in English. Her book *Ukraine's Quest for Identity: Embracing Cultural Hybridity in Literary Imagination, 1991-2011* (2018) is the 2019 winner of the Omeljan Pritsak Book Prize in Ukrainian Studies. Her translations from Polish and Ukrainian have appeared in *Agni, Cyphers, Modern Poetry in Translation, Modern Haiku,* and *Toronto Slavic Annual*. Her most recent book publication is a translated volume of Mykola Vorobiov's selected poetry titled *Mountain and Flower* (2020), which received an honorary mention from the American Association for Ukrainian Studies. Born in Poland to Ukrainian parents, Rewakowicz lives in New York City.

Вірш екологічно-історичний

> *Не говоріте теорій, бо теорія продалася.*
> *Не говоріте нічого – слова то вороги!*
> Юрій Липа

I
коли прикладаю слова
до твоїх уст, Україно,
вони котяться безмовним згустком
по зритих борознах твого лиця

і що нам із тебе
якщо людство
вирізало діру в небі
й сонце таврує нам шкіру

і що нам із тебе
якщо в юшці з двоокису вуглецю
варимо не лише себе,
але й ріки, поля, ліси, моря

і що нам із тебе
якщо замість чистої стрічки повітря
зав'язуємо собі на шиї
намисто кислого дощу

і що нам із тебе
якщо з вершка твоєї голови
зняли зелену рясну чуприну
залишивши сивий чуб
чорнобильського диму...

II
все ж ти ди-хай, ди-хай
вільно, повногрудо, прозоро
вчися вимовляти сонце
кругло, ра-дій-сно, синьо

заплітай тирсі коси в степу,
якщо ще росте,
вимивай лице у Дніпрі,
якщо він ще тече,
любуйся Чорним морем
доки воно ще твоє,
голуби співом ліси,
доки ще зелені...

таки не судилося тобі
натягнути час
на списи століть
історія стала напівдорозі
й мов подряпана пластинка
в старому грамофоні
ікається на звуку у...

previously published in the poetry collection *Zelenyi dakh*
[The Green Roof] (Kyiv: Rodovid, 1999)

Two Monologues

for N.I.

1. Early March Monologue

    night
    snow outside
    white lonely New York
    knocks on the door
    I don't answer
    I wrap myself in your words
    like a warm cozy shawl
    and feel carefree
    it's quiet and still
    just from time to time the street begins to speak
    in a passing car
    in absence there's a certain gravity
    a word not thoroughly explained
    that's hanging above our distance
    you'd like to open this word
    like a book
    and who will guess what's on the final page?
    I'm falling asleep not having read it to the end
    And it's real winter outside the window…

2. Mid-February Monologue

    and why do you need to open the door
    to the entangled past?
    the door has been grated too long
    with the heavy padlock of bygone days
    and a grimly rusted key
    Kyiv in mid-February 2010
    alluring in translucent frost and corrupt politics
    unexpectedly brings your blossoming smile
    as if it is a dessert in a strange bowl out of which
    sham, warmed through by the sun, slides down
    like snow from the sloping roof
    one can chat about everything over a cup of tea
    easiest to talk about politics
    it's cheap and does not oblige
    yet there's no desire to talk about ourselves
    too many winters have flowed to the sea
    too much grass has been burnt in the sun
    though still – why do I want dessert so much?

    Translated from the Ukrainian by Svitlana Bednazh

previously published in *International Poetry Review* (Special Issue: Twenty-Five Years of Ukrainian Poetry) Vol. XXXVI, no. 2 Fall 2010

Oksana Rosenblum is an art history researcher and translator based in New York City. She was born and raised in Ukraine but calls NYC her home since 2003. Her poetry translations from Ukrainian, essays, and book reviews appeared in *National Translation Month*, *Versopolis*, *Ukrainian Weekly*, and *Asymptote*. She co-edited a bilingual volume of the early poetry of Mykola Bazhan, an important and prolific Ukrainian poet of the 20th century (Academic Studies Press, 2020).

Маріанні Кіяновській та Грицькові Чубаю

Так наче щось всередині раптом зламалось –
Чи двигун, чи барометр, чи бог його зна
Вийшло з ладу, зашпорталось
У просторі сну

Ніби частина серця мого відлетіла
З шорохом в кут закотилась
Я ловила руками, губами її ловила
Не знайшла

Ой матінко, що ж воно буде
Ой татусю, куди ж це воно
Двигтить – гримотить – ніжками перебирає
Крильцями тріпоче – поривається
Тупцює – розвертається
Валить – наїжджає – скажено гарчить
Всміхається – по-диявольски зубами клацає
І ди -
   ди –
   ди –
   хати не дає

Наче забулося все що було
Сталось давно й не дуже
Хочу до тебе я друже
Руку свою простягти

Вийшла на ганок я зранку, ой леле
Сукню весільну провідать...
Що ж мені сукня, ой леле,
Коли вже шиються нараменники
Лаштуються гармати
Біда насуває з усіх боків

Летіти лелем по траві древній
Повзти дурепою у тлустій олії
Молитися мовою намарних мжичок
В тилу тулубом тіла
торсати
борсати
клацати
мацати
брязкати
гаркати
нявчааааати
кричааааати
дуріти
марніти
говорити
говорити
гово –
 рити
 рити
 рити
бути
забути
просити?
Благати?
Вимагати?
 Плакати-ридати?

Як це воно? Оце як це? Це як?
Отак
Атак
А так
Танк
Тутбувтанкатак

Там був танк!!
А, так?
Може, так
Może być tak
Może być atak
Psychiczny atak
Tak...

Мовчати.
 спати
  спати
  спати...

"Московскоє врємя – полночь"

Ksenia Rychtycka is a Detroit-based poet and fiction writer whose Ukrainian heritage is often highlighted in her creative work. Her poetry chapbook *A Sky Full of Wings* (Finishing Line Press, 2021), won the Eric Hoffer Book Award in the chapbook category and the da Vinci Eye for cover design. The book was also shortlisted for the Eric Hoffer Award grand prize and was a finalist in the New Women's Voices Chapbook Competition. Her short story collection *Crossing The Border* (Little Creek Books, 2012), was a finalist in the Next Generation Indie Book Awards. Ksenia's work has appeared in *Alaska Quarterly Review*, *The Literary Bohemian*, *Yellow Medicine Review*, *Wisconsin Review*, *The Dalhousie Review* and elsewhere. She worked as an editor in Kyiv during the early years of the post-Soviet era and has backpacked through twelve countries in Europe. Ksenia earned an MA in Creative Writing from Columbia College Chicago.

Watching A Revolution From A Computer Screen
   Ukraine, 2014

Drone of drum, hand over hand,
beat for beat, breath for breath.

Silence as much an illusion as the snake
charmer who plays it up for the crowd.

Slightest curve of hand -- he thinks you're fooled.
Let the snake loose, unfurl the fury.

The coffers have long been bare.
These streets, your streets, my streets

are now covered in blood. What can we do --
here, now -- as black tires flare?

Even the poet has been pummeled.
The screen darkens and still we watch.

        previously published in *A Sky Full of Wings*
        Finishing Line Press, 2022

Slippage

I read aloud to Mother,
enunciating her own words --
the poems she'd stayed up
nights writing after years alone
raising children – velvet
night her muse, her savior.

Mother smiles but sits mute,
stroking my palm. Blue eyes
wander. Already I am losing her.
She wants to go back to her
childhood home in Roznitiv,
live with her mother and father
long gone.

I distract her -- sing off-key,
folk songs we once twirled to
on the linoleum floor of our
compact kitchen, feet stomping
with passion of Hutsul mountain
folk or young couples jumping
bonfires on Midsummer Eve.

Mother hums along, happy.
These songs are in her bones.
These songs have traveled
through blood-stained lands --
sustained her through bombings
and a rough ocean crossing
taking her far -- then farther still
from her childhood home.

Mother doesn't know of the current
war in her homeland, of one hundred
protesters shot dead by snipers
on same square where we danced
on New Year's Eve, of Crimea overrun
on Kremlin's orders, of soldiers

slipping over the Ukrainian border seventy
years after she'd fled all those invaders.

No, Mother doesn't know.
And if only for this –
I am glad.

>	previously published in *A Sky Full of Wings*
>	Finishing Line Press, 2022

Vera Sirota is a poet, freelance writer, and teacher. She was a NYC public school teacher and teaching artist specializing in writing instruction. She wrote her master's thesis about using photography as a writing tool for English Language Learners. Vera was raised in a bilingual and bicultural home as the granddaughter of Ukrainian immigrants. Vera serves as a mentor for Girls Write Now, NYC's premier creative writing organization for high school girls and gender-expansive youth. She is a finalist for The Poetry Barn's 2022 Poetic License contest.

Forsaken

Near the pines
death was everywhere
Bucha butchered

Bodies strewn
rotted stench
desecrated fruit
on Yablonska Street

Among them
Maksym the Fearless
chestnut-eyed shepherd
guided strangers to basements
with wolves at their heels

Found
hands bound
behind his back
a blanket of blood
staining the ground
his final prayer
unanswered
sundered from his flock

The woman who was found naked except for a fur coat locked in a potato cellar shot in the head

I was a little girl, age 6
when my family traveled
for a summer holiday
to Odessa.

I distinctly remember
the ivory columns
of Plyazh Arkadiya
welcoming us.
Donning my favorite emerald bathing suit
I shouted with glee.
I clutched Papa's hand
dashing into the Black Sea.

The waves enveloped my crown
salt seeping into my skin.
I would float for hours
gazing at the seagulls
mesmerized by their melodies
as they danced
in the air
euphoric and free.

Despite all odds

When the air raid siren blares
I remain
defiant
in my bed
on the top floor of my home.
I dare a Moscow missile to find me.

I am 99 years old.
I survived the Nazi invasion
Stalin's terror
Soviet oppressors
now – Putin's pillagers.

Through it all,
I recite the words of
Lesia Ukrainka's "Contra Spem Spero!"

Hope animates my heart
despite all odds
because this is a national trait
a pride that propels us
a song that sustains us.
We bow to no one
and never will.

Virlana Tkacz heads the Yara Arts Group and has directed almost forty original shows at La MaMa in New York that also performed in Kyiv, Lviv, Kharkiv, Bishkek, Ulaanbaatar, and Ulan Ude. She received an NEA Poetry Translation Fellowship for her work with Wanda Phipps on Serhiy Zhadan's poetry. Her production of *1917-2017: Tychyna Zhadan & the Dogs* won the 2018 New York Innovative Theatre Awards for best musical. She is the author of *Three Wooden Trunks,* a book of poetry published this spring.

Tiananmen Square

Today sitting in my East Village apartment
I mourn the deaths of people I do not know,
but who are changing the way we view life
and history.
The demonstrators are calling out,
asking us to say their names.
Yes: George Floyd, Breonna Taylor and Ahmaud Arbery
must be remembered
and must force us to change
the way we look
or don't look
at what is happening around us.
We who supported those who stood
for their rights all winter in the Maydan in Kyiv
with plywood shields against
police with live ammunition
should see the similarities.
Our Heavenly Hundred faced snipers
sent from abroad by a tyrant
who left us his mansion,
black ledger books and golden toilets.
But even today the image of protest
that is seared in my brain
is that of a lone protester standing
in front of a tank
that is trying every maneuver
in the manual to avoid him
in Tiananmen Square.

I saw this moment live
when I was in Quebec City in 1989
for a conference of Slavic Scholars.
For the first time ever we had guests
from the Soviet Union with us:
Les Taniuk and Nelli Kornienko.
Romana Bahriy and I had invited them
with no hope of ever seeing them.
But then they unexpectedly arrived
and their appearance overwhelmed us.
We were broke, to put it mildly.
But they went along, always gracious.
As we sat in a cheap Chinese restaurant
we were all mesmerized
by the footage on the news
that needed no translation.
One of the waitresses suddenly
broke down in hysterical tears.
She must of recognized someone
or maybe knew someone who was in the Square.
We all froze.
It was Nelli Kornienko, who grew up in Siberia,
that alone stood up and embraced her,
assuring her, in Ukrainian, that we all felt her pain
and were willing to stand with her
and the students in Tiananmen Square.
As she rocked the sobbing waitress in her embrace
I started to believe in a new Ukraine.
We too could become a people
who could see beyond our own victim-hood
to become big enough
to identify with the hurt of others.
We too could then
join the fight for what is right.

Currently a writer and visual artist, **Christina Turczyn** has contributed watercolors to twenty exhibits including Cornell Has Talent. In her career as a writer, she has over one hundred publications in diverse magazines and journals. Those span international events covered at the Guggenheim, and The World Around Summit. She is a member of the Women's Foreign Policy Group.

Elsewhere

I come for the deer--
this season, they kick up snow
in circles,
summoning clouds,
an ancient path of constellations
in the blood.

"Let your body remember," my Tai Chi
master reminds me, as scars
are a calligraphy of absence.

It is all in the breath:
Geography of skin.
What we know is on the other
side of bone.

Here, the pandemic creates silence,
prolongs the wait. I am
hurried out of the hospital, and still
am happy for the twentysomething,
who forgot to go to work, then arrived
after too much wine.

The nurses keep
laughing, but his friend comes to take
him home.
No one would do this for them,
as they
miss the secret--

undercurrent, stone.

Elsewhere in cages children go quietly to sleep,
without any knowledge of the depth
that being held up by a river brings.

Today, the deer summon a storm.
They thunder through the woods,
white water,
just listening.

Winter Coat

Leaving the camp,
a mother takes her daughter by the hand.
They walk along the path toward school.
A warm sleeve of wind envelops her,
until cold weather comes.
First the pain.
Then the numbness.
Then the education.
Walking past the distant hills, she feels
bread in the heart,
hunger in the heart of bread—
counts deer tracks, sees
galaxies of deer circling mountains,
life scaling stone.

Bucha

The doors are gone
beneath a cloud's turning script.
Enter the children, stones,
giving voice to streams.
Enter the woman caught between arrival
and arrival.
To be trapped between the body and infinity—
breath and sky.
What is a life without doors?
Just a notion dividing
yesterday and yesterday--
This and that.
A quiet leaving, heard by no one.
A rape.
A face turned to the wall.
Who will wear her shadow?
Who will free her voice,
caught as it is, a bird in the throat?
In war, what is worse--
The blinding memory of love or burial,
death or its absence,
blood or light?

Genya Turovskaya was born in Kyiv, Ukraine, and grew up in New York City. She is the author of *The Breathing Body of This Thought* (Black Square Editions) as well as numerous chapbooks. Her poetry has appeared in Asymptote, Chicago Review, Conjunctions, Fence, PEN Poetry Series, Pocket Samovar, Sangam Poetry, Seedings, The Elephants, and other publications. She has received a Fund for Poetry Grant, a MacDowell Colony Fellowship, a Montana Artist Refuge Fellowship, a Witter Bynner Translation Residency at Santa Fe Art Institute, and a Whiting Award. She lives in New York City where she is a practicing psychotherapist.

The Late Arrival (Another New Year`s Day)

The soldiers did not have adequate training to complete the mission

Since nothing had taken place, nothing was lost, nothing needed to be recovered

The child plays quietly underfoot, her mind rippling with the gentle rhythm of its babble

The girl remained as a feeling, through her arrival a portal can open

I have trouble staying awake tangled in blue swaddling on a black couch in a too-spacious room

Boredom is a symptom, an anhedonia, a lusterless ocean

The water's surface is briefly troubled by a breeze or the fart of some marine creature

The mind, before language, an animal presence

Through her animal presence the girl remains, insistent, as hope is the heart's property

Mine was a forced entry

I have always been the late arrival, my mothers labor induced

I have not been possibly or impossibly on nodding terms with the reckless astonishment

The collision out of which life, out of which irrevocable life

And at that moment, as her mind is elsewhere, the blazing child twists out of her mothers grasp

Whose mind is it, anyway?

A person made out of ash and air, a passionate refusal, a requiem, the requisite wreaths of red carnations, tiered, cake-like

A man shows off his rope tricks, lassos a utility pole, and the rope in his hand becomes a live wire

When does the crowd observing the spectacle become aware that they are watching a man die?

Are you too a failed witness?

Now that I know what to do will I do it?

I am always returning to reunion, running parallel to refusal, requiem, boredom

The girl remains, conceives herself, her mind

A live wire

The crowd disperses, filling in the grid of the streets and avenues

Did I refuse my own arrival?

The labor-inducing drug is called Pitocin, a flood, synthetic, of oxytocin, the labor described as "excruciating"

There were only mothers at the birthing house, no fathers allowed

I had an aerial view of the city and black water slowly rose and filled in the grid of the streets and avenues

Or was it smoke? Ash and air?

The portal through which she arrives, and the portal that through her will open, a harbor, a silvering skyline

At the birthing house red-faced infants were held up to windows, the fathers, when there were fathers, stood outside in the snow, clutching red carnations, red roses

Soluble thoughts

The train pulls in to the station and the connecting train pulls in and the doors open in near simultaneity and stay open exactly long enough to cross the platform from one train to the other

This can be a form of happiness, a consolation, this alignment, this need to be met and carried from one place to another

I slept too long and woke sad with the residue of a dream I couldn't remember except that it was sexual

I was too late

Something stood in the way of some other thing, I lost my shoes, recovered my lost shoes and immediately lost them again

There were too many rooms, there was no room in which to be alone together

Something was amiss, the gulls were too far inland or the ocean was too far inland

Boredom is the swaddling blue ocean, synthetic, a symptom, or the necessary condition for the mind's labor, for the passing breeze

You can't force reunion — soldier, compliant and pliable — even with yourself

The gummy toothlessness of the very young and the very old is disquieting

Crust of drool silvering on the chin, all of our liquid secretions assuming solid form

All that is liquid in ourselves

All the spillage of our soluble thoughts filling in the grid

All the preludes and the lewd exertions

All of the late arrivals are sequestered, made to watch the opera televised on a screen in an anteroom

The sweat of the singers exertions is beaded on their brows, you can almost see the vapor of the air forced lung-shaped out of their mouths

What consumes you?

Fear of abandonment, electrocution, the swallowed and swallowing ocean, of belonging to oneself only, insolvency in old age

The mission was a reconnaissance, the soldiers did not have a soldier's constitution

The medication is administered as a sublingual lozenge, as an intravenous drip, as a suppository

You have been instructed not to forget, not to gorge on the oxytocin of reunion, to soldier onward

The mind will fill in the intervals between x and y with its unreliable testimony

O frigates on the rising ocean! O foregoing!

Am I too late?

My frog voice cracks

How does a soldier acquire a soldier's constitution?

A word is made first of sound, incendiary, the meaning follows

> previously published in *The Breathing Body of This Thought*
> Black Square Editions

Nicole Yurcaba (Ukrainian: Нікола Юрцаба) is a Ukrainian American poet, novelist and essayist. Her poems and essays have appeared in *The Atlanta Review, The Lindenwood Review, Whiskey Island, Raven Chronicles, Appalachian Heritage, North of Oxford,* and many other online and print journals. Nicole holds an MFA in Writing from Lindenwood University, and she teaches poetry workshops for Southern New Hampshire University and works as a career counselor for Blue Ridge Community College. She is a guest book reviewer for *Sage Cigarettes, Tupelo Quarterly, Colorado Review,* and *The Southern Review of Books.*

i write for you & only you
my beloved *ukrayina*
where in my dreams
i sleep i live i die
in old age   my head
resting on an embroidered pillow
i crafted in my youth
when i laughed in lviv
      loved in odessa
        stood staring at the sky
           in kolomyia
  heard my grandfather whisper

                              you're here

You're playing Lemko songs again:
those songs that sing our souls
home to an ancient tongue
twisting our lips one onto the other's
& i imagine the lath fence
where you find me blushing & barefoot
a smudge of dirt on my embroidered blouse
a tingle of sweat on your dark brow
a sideways glance cast down the wagon road
to make sure no one's coming
         & oh my sweetheart
you take my hand   lace my farm-weary fingers
into yours & with no words you tell me
Marichka, my Marichka!
Tall & dark Marichka!
My Marichka, let me declare my intentions
to your aging father!
& i see the embroideries
         the wedding table spread
open blank pages across our Carpathian sky
where god & fate & forest spirits
tightknit our souls–two into one
         & oh my darling
i'm dreaming again
of a history hidden in our eyes
& those songs you play on repeat
as bombs erase apartment buildings
& tanks prowl broken villages
& soldiers deliver fresh-baked bread
to a mother waving goodbye to her only son
& another infant dies in a storm of fire & steel
& a father falls to his knees beside his daughter's grave
& yes my darling
someday i'll find you at the elm tree,
my eyes as dark as black berries
         & we'll marry on a Sunday
                 in the presence of god
                 the absence of war
                         –i hope

someday we'll tell the children
--for I.K.W.

how we met during the war
ripping our ancestral homeland
the way grandmother's dress tore
in a german soldier's hands
eighty years ago   revealing her thin ribs
the rose-bruised skin   to chilled open air
before grandfather emerged from behind the barn
tiptoed through the trampled yard
a pitchfork his father made raised high
& pierced the soldier's back until maroon tainted gray

someday you'll tell the children
how many times i called you
crying after Bucha's wounds revealed the bodies:
we both knew too well
what lies buried in mass graves
   housed in camps
   the pain we carry within the very marrow
the enemy attempted to suck from
the high cheek bones of our daughter's face
the broad shoulders of our son

& someday I'll tell them
how the morning after it snowed
i spent 30 minutes in a chilly farmhouse bathroom
listening to the U2 song you sent the night before
after i'd fallen asleep   alone again
reading a Tokarczuk novel & i sent you
Lutsyshyna verses with the caveat
*I know too well what she means about the peasants
after all my last name means "farmer"* & i speak
that nearly extinct carpatho-rusyn tongue
our children learned because i insisted

but before we tell them the story behind our stories
they'll see you look up from the book you're reading
when i walk into the room wearing your faded flannel shirt

& they'll hear how i laugh when we're cooking dinner
& your hand touches mine when you're reaching
for the cast-iron skillet mamo & tato bought us–a housewarming
gift along with the *rushnyk* bearing two swans
                                    two interlocked rings
                                    the words of our destiny
            embroidered on white in fiery red

DONATE

Razom for Ukraine

https://www.razomforukraine.org/donate/

DONATE

Serhiy Zhadan Charitable Foundation

https://www.razomforukraine.org/projects/zhadan/

WATCH THE VIRTUAL EVENT

Ukrainian American Poets Respond Reading March 16, 2022

Ukrainian American Poets Respond Reading April 14, 2022

www.ingramcontent.com/pod-product-compliance
Lightning Source LLC
Chambersburg PA
CBHW020541080526
44583CB00013B/945